BBC Children's Books
Published by the Penguin Group
Penguin Books Ltd, 80 Strand, London, WC2R 0RL, England
Penguin Group (Australia) Ltd, 250 Camberwell Road, Camberwell, Victoria
3124, Australia (a division of Pearson Australia Group Pty Ltd)
Canada, India, New Zealand, South Africa

Published by BBC Children's Books, 2010
Text and design © Children's Character Books, 2010
This edition produced for The Book People ltd, Hall Wood Avenue,
Haydock, St Helens, WA11 9UL

10 9 8 7 6 5 4 3 2

Written by Gillian Hutchison
Designed by Dan Newman, Perfect Bound Ltd

ISBN: 978-1-40590-770-5

Printed in Italy

Contents

Who are the Top Gear Team?

THIS MAN loves nothing more than driving expensive cars and describing them in a way that can sometimes make you feel a bit confused. His favourite hobby is winning challenges, even if it means bending the rules just a little. There's absolutely nothing wrong with sabotaging other *Top Gear* team members' cars is there? Thought not.

THIS MAN loves nothing more than a Porsche. Or a supercharged car. Or a supercharged, super expensive car and a blocked-off mile of road to drive it at top speed on. He even likes two-wheeled vehicles called 'motorcycles'. If they have a special name he pretends he's a superhero with special powers. And yes, we promise he is old enough to drive.

> It's the only car I've *ever* driven ever which is a **killer attack dog** *and* an **old sofa**.

> Ray Montague Smythe had a *deadly* secret, for he was… the **Black Shadow!**

Mmm, tools in drawer!

THIS MAN loves nothing more than explaining to his *Top Gear* teammates exactly and precisely how things work. Especially when they are not interested in knowing. But he has a vast amount of knowledge up in his well-covered, hairy head and he wants to let it out! He is not biased towards fast cars and likes all four-wheeled vehicles on their individual merit. Especially if they have GPS and allow him not to get lost.

I believe I won!

HE IS *Top Gear*'s tame racing driver. Some say he thought *Star Wars* was a documentary and that he's scared of bells. Some say that it's impossible for him to wear socks and to unlock him you have to run your finger down his face. What we do know is, when he walks, his feet make a guitar wah-wah noise and one of his legs is hydraulic. We also know that he has a swivelling head and when he blinks, you can hear a noise like a camera shutter. Just who is he exactly? Turn the page to find out!

The STIG REVEALED!

The Stig's identity – revealed on *Top Gear*? Never! But The Stig had had enough of the rumours circulating on the news and the Internet and decided to do something he had not done before. He decided to reveal his head. In the studio.

IT WAS a very, very exciting moment. The Stig has always been full of surprises, so what do you think happened when he sat down with Jeremy? He decided not to remove his helmet! The anticipation was dashed and Jeremy had to do some serious convincing to talk him into it. Luckily, it worked. And all was revealed.

The Stig… is… *Michael Schumacher!*

Jeremy immediately got down to the nitty gritty by asking the big questions that we've all been pondering for years.

You've got a head! *Ears!* You've got **everything!**

This is *obviously* a **big moment**. My heart's fluttering.

Are you illegal in seventeen US states?

No, no, it's **much** too exaggerated. It's only **nine**.

Some people have told us that you only know **two** facts about ducks and both of them are *wrong*. Is that true?

Well, I mean, *obviously* they don't fly...

You're right. You don't know **anything** about ducks.

Now we know. It's true. The Stig *can* be wrong about some things. Luckily he knows how to stick to the facts about cars, roads and power lap times.

The conversation took a serious turn when Jeremy asked Michael if he finds it a bit boring watching races when one driver endlessly wins race after race after race after race. It was definitely something Michael could relate to. No wonder the power lap times are so good. Everything now makes sense. Phew. Now we can relax.

Or is he?

So... maybe Michael Schumacher really isn't The Stig!

It was time for him to make 'Star in a Reasonably-Priced Car' history and blast Lewis Hamilton and every other star off the board.
Here we go:

BRRMM BRRUMM BRUUH—

KOFF-KADUGGA-DUGGA

Uh oh. His start wasn't the best. He stalled. Michael Schumacher STALLED the Liana!

SCREEE!!

Into Chicago Corner and things didn't really go well. Off the track and straight towards a *Top Gear* cameravan!

Nor did the windscreen. Bashed and broken, the Liana powered on to the follow-through... at a leisurely pace. What was going on?

He was going the wrong way! But he might recover for the final corner...

ZZZzzzzzzzrrrrrr! Crunch! Crunch! went the gears once he managed to get going. What was happening?

But, he managed to recover and get back on the track.

KKRNTCH

First corner and the white line disappears under the tyres as he heads straight over it and into the grass.

POW

The cameraman made it to safety in the nick of time. Sadly, the camera didn't.

Ah no. Michael Schumacher never finished the race!

Michael Schumacher is *lost*, everybody!

Don't Miss!

A lot of seventeen-year-olds have a few little accidents when they begin to drive.

Jeremy, Richard and James loved pretending they were teenagers again (which was before television was even invented) when they were set the challenge of hitting every obstacle in their affordable first cars. Follow the maze and make sure you crash through each obstacle before reaching the end.

That was **strangely** satisfying.

Start ▶

Finish

CLANG!

Know Your Supercars?

Oh! What a *noise!*

Lamborghini and Ferrari never fail to impress each year with supercharged, super expensive supercars.

They sometimes leave the *Top Gear* chaps speechless, but never with any doubt about where these machines should be positioned on the Cool Wall. How well do you know your Lambos and Ferraris? Take the quiz below to find out.

1 **This Lambo was deemed uncool by both Jeremy and Richard. Which one was it?**
a) Lamborghini Murciélago LP670-4 SV
b) Lamborghini Gallardo
c) Lamborghini Gumbopesto

2 **What Lamborghini did Richard drive through the blocked-off streets of Abu Dhabi?**
a) Lamborghini 640 Roadster
b) Lamborghini Murciélago LP670- 4 SV
c) Lamborghini Reventón

3 **A new Lamborghini is named after a test driver. What was his name?**
a) Francesco Tortoni
b) Valentino Balboni
c) Ken Shufflebottom

4 **Which Ferrari was removed from the Power Lap board for having slick tyres?**
a) Ferrari FXX
b) Ferrari Spyder
c) Ferrari Gallardo

5 **How many people who pre-ordered the F430 Scuderia Spider will feel pretty silly when they see the new Ferrari 458 Italia?**
a) 99
b) 499
c) 450

6 **What is the fastest Ferrari on the Power Lap board?**
a) Ferrari Enzo
b) Ferrari 360 CS
c) Ferrari Scuderia

Reasonably Fast Stars

Who is the fastest star in the reasonably-priced Chevrolet Lacetti? Answer the questions about the celebs below to spell out the name of the fastest star. For extra points, guess the time of the fastest lap.

1 Who is the mayor of London?

2 Who is the fastest man in the world?

3 Who recently made a movie about Sherlock Holmes, released in December 2009?

4 This singer is named after the travel sickness he suffers from. What is his name?

5 What is the surname of the actor who played the Tenth Doctor in *Doctor Who*?

6 This comedian spun off the *Top Gear* track and is the very last on the board. What is his name?

Circle the fastest lap time.

1.42.3   1.45.8   1.46.1   1.47.5

Kenny from the Block

Ken Block prefers to use airfields instead of racetracks to sharpen his driving skills in his Subaru Impreza rally car. There's just a few things he has to watch out for when he's practising. See if you can find them in the word search below.

A	T	R	H	G	Y	R	F	C	V	E	D
N	E	O	M	O	T	O	R	B	I	K	E
B	G	R	F	D	E	R	T	Y	U	I	J
M	S	R	O	O	D	Q	C	X	Z	G	U
N	H	E	K	P	H	T	L	Y	H	B	N
R	F	V	M	B	L	H	R	W	D	R	K
F	H	U	E	A	W	A	K	E	O	P	Y
Z	J	V	G	T	J	N	N	Q	S	F	A
T	Y	B	V	C	D	G	S	E	W	E	R
Q	C	G	T	H	Y	A	A	B	S	E	D
R	Y	A	W	N	U	R	Q	W	C	F	H
F	I	R	E	S	T	A	T	I	O	N	B

Aeroplanes
Desert
Doors
Fire station
Hangar
James

Jump
Junkyard
Motorbike
Runway

Mod Your Ride

What's the best method to make modifications to your car on the cheap? Pile them on! Too much is never enough!

Jeremy, Richard and James showed their *Top Gear* enthusiasm when adding extras to their seventeen-year-old boy cars.

Extra bodywork to make it streamlined and sporty.

CRUNCH!!!

WARNING!

Don't forget about your bodykit when crossing muddy fields.

We literally have to glue the *whole* thing. *Every* button.

WARNING!

Keep your car away from Jeremy and Richard. And glue.

I've added a *bangin' stereo* for me tunes.

The biggest sound system you can afford.

DUNGA DUNGA DUNGA DUNGA DUNGA

TSSH-TSSH-TSSH-TSSH-TSSH-TSSH-TSSH-TSSH-TSSH-TSSH-TSSH-TSSH-TSSH-TSSH-TSSH

A DUNGA DUNGA DUNGA DUNGA

START

VRRAOM

The Fast and the Confused

On a racetrack in France, the trio thought it would be a piece of cake to beat The Stig's lap time in a front-wheel drive Twingo. After all, they all had rear-wheel drives. And a bit of attitude. How hard could it be?

Pity they didn't know the track that well. Find your way to the finish line by following the yellow line to find a route through the maze.

LOSER!

What?! But I was going like hell!

LOSER!

That *didn't* go as well as I'd hoped.

LOSER!

WINNER!

FINISH

MEAN MACHINES!

Jeremy had a game of British Bulldogs with some scary-looking vehicles from the army. Jeremy was in a modified Mitsubishi Evo VII RS and he had to make sure he avoided the live ammunition. Match the pictures with the names below.

Jackal

Mastiff PPV

Trojan

Panther

Titan AVLB

A

B

C

D

E

Race to the North

The *Top Gear* team stepped back in time to 1949 to see who would win a race to the North.

A

Jeremy was in a Tornado steam train, James in a Jaguar XK120 and Richard on a Vincent Black Shadow motorbike. Who would win? Jeremy gave it his best, shovelling coal as fast as he could to make the locomotive huff and puff all the way to Edinburgh. See if you can pick out twelve differences between pictures A and B.

B

Bugatti Veyron

Power Lap POWER!

Do you know your Power Lap times as well as The Stig? Below are some of the top-ten fastest times round the TG track.

See if you can match the times with a few of the fastest production cars in the world. It's a tricky one, but if The Stig can do it… surely you can too.

Pagani Zonda F Roadster

Gumpert Apollo

Ascari A10

Caterham R500

Koenigsegegggsegg CCX
(with Top Gear spoiler)

1.17.1	. . . .
1.17.3	. . . .
1.17.6	. . . .
1.17.8	. . . .
1.17.9	. . . .
1.18.3	. . . .

Supercharged Supercars

> You'd have to be **bonkers** to buy the Corvette. And that is why you **should**.

Corvette ZR1

Even though this easily beat the Audi R8 in a drag race, Jeremy still wasn't really impressed with the Corvette. It's sort of plasticky on the inside and out, and only available in left-hand drive. Then on the track when you take it to the corners, it behaves like a crazy person – more crazy than Jeremy. So this makes for a nerve-wracking drive when there is more power than a Ferrari Enzo bursting to get out.

Engine: Supercharged V8

Power: 638 bhp

0-60 mph: 3.3 seconds

Top speed: 205 mph

TG power lap: 1 min 20.4 seconds

Audi R8

Jeremy loved this car so much he licked it. Yes. Right on the steering wheel. He not only loved the power and prowess, but also the practical design features like being able to fit into the car comfortably and even put maybe three small goats in the boot. That's just what every supercar needs. Room to put your goats.

Engine: *Lamborghini V10*

Power: *518 bhp*

0-60 mph: *3.7 seconds*

Top speed: *200 mph*

TG power lap: *1 min 21.6 seconds*

VRROOOMM

It does 150 to 170 *so quickly* your eyeballs bounce in the back of your skull like *squash balls.*

Noble M600

This little old car made in deepest Leicestershire is no-frills. There's no satnav, no climate control, no airbags and no anti-lock brakes. But in terms of speed, it can blow all the other supercharged supercars out of the water. So, really, what more could you ask for in a supercar? Who really needs things like anti-lock brakes? As long as you're The Stig, there should be no problems at all.

Engine: *Turbocharged V8*

Power: *650 bhp*

0-60 mph: *3 seconds*

Top speed: *225 mph*

TG power lap: *1 min 17.7 seconds*

It's even got a spoiler! It's the *real deal.*

Lexus LFA

So when Lexus announced they were releasing a sports car, oh how they laughed and guffawed in the *Top Gear* office. But then, oh, how they ate humble pie for breakfast, lunch and dinner. It's up there in power, speed and style with Ferraris, Lambos and Aston Martins. Not bad for a first try. It's ridiculously, ludicrously expensive though and it is still a Lexus.

Engine: V10

Power: 552 bhp

0-60 mph: 3.7 seconds

Top speed: 202 mph

TG power lap: 1 min 22.8 seconds

Lamborghini Gallardo LP 550-2 Valentino Balboni

This was the perfect car to take on a caravanning holiday with James. Especially when the caravan didn't have to be towed. Richard didn't even complain about the fact that he had to go on a caravanning holiday while he was driving the stripped-back version of the Lambo. The basic gearbox and rear-wheel drive were enough to keep him happy. And the fact that James was miles above him in the sky, floating around in a caravan airship.

Engine: V10

Power: 540 bhp

Top speed: 199 mph

0-60 mph: 3.9 seconds

TG power lap: not tested

So You Think You Know Your Cars?

A

Jeremy's job is pretty cool. He gets to drive super expensive cars around a track and talk about them.

But have you been paying attention? Take a look at the mixed-up model names below and see if you can work out the real names and then match them to the right picture. Pretty easy? Good luck!

1: RUDIA8

— — — —   — —

2: BMXM5W

— — —   — — —

3: BLOMOONE6

— — — — —   — — — —

4: TERVORCTEIZ

— — — — — — —   — — —

5: 6XWBM

— — —   — —

6: DIQ7UA

— — — — —   — —

B

C

D

E

F

OY58 FXW

So, Captain **Cautious**, what are you going to do **now**?

Classic Car Challenge

This was going to be a fun challenge. The *Top Gear* team had to buy classic cars.

Then they were told they had to compete in one big challenge rather than a series of small ones. As many hold the opinion that classic cars are way more fun than new cars, they were pretty intrigued – most of these classic car enthusiasts also liked birdwatching and wearing slacks. How much fun could it be?

		TRUE	FALSE
1	Jeremy, Richard and James had £2,000 to buy a car that was built before 1982.	☐	☐
2	Richard shocked James and Jeremy by buying the first V8 car that appeared in the auction. Anything sort of supercharged will do.	☐	☐
3	Jeremy's car wasn't quite the right size for him. He had to take the roof off to squash himself in.	☐	☐
4	James' car was so old that he had to wear driving goggles and gloves because it had no windscreen.	☐	☐
5	Jeremy thought his challenge couldn't go any smoother. Especially when he met his assistant driver, a British rally car champion.	☐	☐
6	James took a less than impressive 31.7 seconds to reach 0-60 mph in his Citroën.	☐	☐
7	Some parts of the race in Majorca involved travelling at a specified speed. It's a shame James' speedometer didn't work.	☐	☐
8	James was not impressed when his assistant driver decided to do some hair-styling while he was driving.	☐	☐
9	Richard and James sabotaged Jeremy's car by jamming the heating on at full strength.	☐	☐
10	Jeremy managed to amass the greatest number of rally points in history. This was not a good thing.	☐	☐

Some of Those Other Cars That Aren't Supercars...

For some of us unfortunate ones, owning a supercar one day is but a dream. So we'll have to make do with other types of cars. Like sedans, coupés, hatchbacks or even a rally car would do. Come on, they're not all bad! Well, some of them aren't anyway.

> The X6 is *too cramped* and too complicated.

BMW X6

Jeremy didn't quite know what to make of this car, so he had to take a little trip to Sydney, Spain, the Alps, Hong Kong and Barbados to see if he could make up his mind. And he did. He didn't like it. It's not a good road car and not a good off-road car. It's just not much good.

Engine: Inline 6

Power: 302 bhp

Top speed: 150 mph

0-60 mph: 6.7 seconds

YC58 RXA

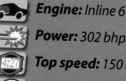

Vauxhall Insignia VXR

This has a very special button that James liked. When you pressed 'sport' and then 'VXR', the instrument panel turned red! But it also suited James' sensible side (which is most of him) with its look and feel. He thought even a chav would wear their baseball hat the right way round when driving it.

Engine: turbocharged V6

Power: 321 bhp

Top speed: 170 mph

0-60 mph: 5.8 seconds

It's a *fire-breathing monster* with a spine of iron.

Renault Sport Twingo 133

Jeremy conquered a bout of man-cold to race this little fiery Twingo against a Fiat 500 Abarth. And it lost. But it's cheaper than a 500 and it's comfortable to drive, especially if you want to drive upside down in a sewage tunnel in Belfast and afterwards launch yourself and the car (and Ross Kemp) into the sea.

Engine: *1.6L*

Power: *133 bhp*

Top speed: *125 mph*

0-60 mph: *8.7 seconds*

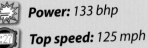

Range Rover 2010 MY

Unlike other supposed off-road vehicles, this one not only goes off-road but it has magical features. Like five cameras where you can view how fast you are approaching obstacles, such as a *Top Gear* camera team, for instance. Lucky for them they realised that, with Jeremy driving, they had to get out of the way.

 Engine: V8 supercharged

Power: 503 bhp

Top speed: 140 mph

0-60 mph: 6.2 seconds

ARRRGGH!

SPALOOSSHH

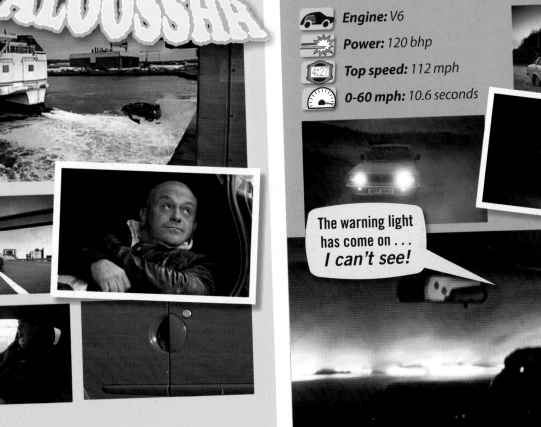

Lancia Beta HPE 2000 IE

Jeremy, Richard and James are convinced that Lancia is the best car company in the world. So to prove it, Jeremy drove the HPE against Richard in a Morris Marina on a rally track for twenty-four hours. But then the Marina had another one of those unfortunate piano-dropping incidents. So even though it caught fire, the Lancia won. Lancia really is the best!

Engine: V6

Power: 120 bhp

Top speed: 112 mph

0-60 mph: 10.6 seconds

The warning light has come on . . . *I can't see!*

Brakes and Burn-outs

Top Gear were pretty excited when they got to do a drag race between the two fastest production cars in the world. It was a world first, too.

Now, here's a game for you to play. Use two counters and a die to make your way up the speedometer readings. Just don't hit the brakes or you'll be going backwards. Hit the burn-outs and you'll be zooming forwards. Good luck!

Brakes

Burn-outs

0 5 10 15 20 25 30 35 40 45 50 55 60 65 70 75 80 85 90 95 100 105 110 115 120 125 130 135 140 145 150 155 160

What I shall do now is climb *out* of the McLaren F1 and climb *into* the Bugatti Veyron. Not a bad day so far.

65 170 175 180 185 190 195 200 205 210 215 220 225 230 235 240 245 250 255 260 265 270 275 280 285 290 295 300 305 310 315 320

How Hard Can it Be?

START

Richard and James were given the challenge of racing a letter all the way from the bottom of England to Scotland.

They were in a Porsche Panamera, the letter was making its way via its usual, mysterious routes. Really. How hard could it be to beat a letter? Find the right path through the maze without doubling back, and you will pass letters that spell out a sentence.

S
L
Y
O
O
R   U   B
T
S
A
O   T
E
L
T
O
L   E
P
T   R

FINISH

I ___ ____ __ _ _____.

Who Said THAT?

The *Top Gear* team are known for their outlandish, strange and sometimes blatantly untrue statements. Can you pick who said what from the quotes below? Draw a line to the presenter you think exclaimed, shouted or guffawed.

I'm going to *change gear* now. This will involve *man-touching.*

We then decided to bring a bit of sCIENCE to the party.

I've got my **head** in a plastic box and *everyone* can see me!

Car makers can learn from this simple system I have adopted.

That is the *worst-looking car* in the whole world.

What I'm doing here is helping realise a **dream** held by many great men.

It's like swimming over a waterfall of *double cream.*

A

B

C

D

E

F

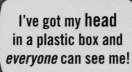

Where on Earth is Transfăgărăşan?

Jeremy, James and Richard were presented with the challenge of driving around Romania on the hunt to find one of the world's best driving roads.

When James was in charge of directions, things didn't go so well. But they found it in the end. Can you find all the words in the word search below?

> By driving around in a Lambo, you're *actually* doing the world a **favour**.

```
T N E I C A L I F O R N I A
L R Q R S T W O R E D N A S
O P A O R S C L M N O J E R
W I P N R R P O R S C H E A
O O T R S A C E G I R K M S
D Q S U W F E R R A R I X T
R Z M L Y G A X U N J A M O
A L A M B O R G H I N I E N
L E J A D R A H A C I R S M
L R E M Y J C A R R F E R A
A S T I N M U R T I A B U R
G S P Y D E R Q T S P S L T
M L O A Y V O L A N T E A I
B D F H J L N S T F L M O N
```

Transfagarasan
Maniya
Jaguar
Porsche
Ferrari
Sandero
Lamborghini
Gallardo
Spyder
California
Aston Martin
Volante

Fancy a Game of Squares?

How easy can it be to make and design an electric car from scratch?

Surely not that hard, thought the *Top Gear* team. After many late nights they produced their very own electric car that ended up looking like… a shiny square box sort of thing.

It looks like a **fish**. A really *square* fish with **wooden ears**.

Instructions:

1 Ask a friend to play with you.

2 Take turns drawing one line between two dots. Do not draw diagonally.

3 Once you have made a square, write your initial in the box.

4 If you complete a square, you get another go to draw a line.

5 At the end of the game, count up and see how many squares you have made. Whoever has the most squares wins.

Player One:

Player Two:

Top Gear ♥ ♥ ♥ Morris Marinas

The Morris Marina Owners' Club seems to have misunderstood *Top Gear*'s dislike for the Marina.

It's not as if *Top Gear* **hate** the Marina. That's reserved for the Volkswagen Beetle. The Marina just doesn't make the top of the 'wish list' for Christmas. And has also happened to have had some bad luck when appearing on the show.

Morris Marina Piano Accident

To ensure they didn't upset any viewers, particularly the Morris Marina lovers, *Top Gear* bought a very fine-looking example of a Marina to preserve for prosperity. Unfortunately it was squashed in a freak helicopter piano removalist accident. **Smash! Splat!** Just like that. It was no more.

> I'll *guarantee* that nothing exciting, vibrant, dynamic, new, creative, hopeful or beneficial in any way to humanity has *ever* been done, thought of or driven to in that drab, dreary, entirely beige, wilfully *awful* pile of misery.

CRASH

> How unlucky was that?!

> Oh, come on, it's not so bad. Umm . . . it's well-equipped. No, it isn't well-equipped, to be honest.

WHAM!

Morris Marina used as Backup Car

What seemed an effortlessly easy challenge ended in disaster for the Marina. The £1,500 rear-wheel drive caused James no end of hassle and he had to jump ship to the Marina. But that meant he was doing very well in the last challenge during a snow race. And James won! But sadly in another freak piano accident, the Marina was squashed.

> That suits you.

Morris Marina as comparison

Top Gear love Lancias, but they have a terrible reputation for being unreliable and shonky. Jeremy set out to drive a tatty 1982 Lancia non-stop through the night on a rally stage. To provide a fair comparison, Richard drove at the same time on the same track (NB: not racing at all, honest) in a Marina of the same age. And, cleverly, to avoid getting a piano on the roof, he bought a car with one attached already. It didn't work. And then the Lancia caught fire.

BA-DOOM

South America or Bust!

It's not a crocodile, it's a lump of wood.

There's a *crocodile* over there!

DAY ONE

Like all challenges, this seemed rather straight-forward. Buy a used four-wheel drive off a Bolivian website and head to Spider Town – a village right next to the Amazon rainforest.

The helicopter that was chartered was going to deliver Jeremy, Richard and James right to where they needed to be … but unfortunately it crashed. So, they found themselves on a tiny boat being amazed by all the wonders of the Amazon. Purple trees! Crocodiles! Butterflies the size of bats! And a fish – possibly a piranha – jumped into the boat so Jeremy stabbed it with his knife. What an intrepid frontier man!

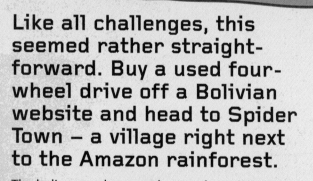

It's *not* a piranha, they're long and thin.

No, they're not!

I'm **sure** there's spiders in here. There will be.

The boat deposited them on the banks of this dangerous river and left them to fend for themselves. Luckily, James had a boot polish kit strapped to his special survivor belt which no one was allowed to touch. Everything was going to be fine.

Richard then confessed that he had a phobia of insects. And he was with Jeremy and James and in the middle of the Amazon. How was this going to go for him?

Is this Batman? No, it's James

The 4WDs were delivered and the team were presented with their challenge – drive through Bolivia to the Pacific Ocean. A mere 1,000 miles away. There would only be a few obstacles, such as an impenetrable jungle, active volcanoes, lifeless deserts and dangerous mountain passes. Obviously no problems ahead.

But before they even began, they would have to try and get their cars off the raft.

And there was the first problem. Jeremy began to sink into the ooze of the Amazon river. Luckily, with the help of the Range Rover, he was rescued – but his jeans were ruined. And still no progress on the car removal.

Hee! Hee! Hee! Look! He's *sinking!*

Now *that's* what I call 4WD!

DAY TWO

The next morning they managed to get the cars on to dry land and they were finally on their way through the jungle. When they made camp, Jeremy entertained Richard with stories of the killer insects of the jungle. Richard surely had a peaceful night's sleep?

James quite liked hacking a path through the trees...

Ergh! What is that? There's something in here *squeaking* at me!

DAY THREE

There were LOTS of bugs. And in the morning Richard found a snake in his car!

DOOFF

How to cross a dry river bed

They battled through the jungle for two days and things went swimmingly – especially when James and Jeremy nearly got stranded in a creek crossing. Eventually they cleared the trees and began rumbling along rocky, rocky roads.

I've bought the only *malfunctioning* Land Cruiser in the world which makes it unique and therefore *priceless*.

DAY FOUR

Oh, I'm so *sick* of that noise! Stop *rattling* at me!

James is *killing* Jeremy. Things are going well.

Huge Drop   Jeremy

After cracking their backs back into place, the team headed on to the most dangerous road in the world, aptly named Death Road. And James was scared. His fear of heights would be a challenge for this treacherous climb with no guardrails. James' fear turned to anger when Jeremy gave him a friendly 4WD bump, so he poked a machete through Jeremy's window to get him back.

Somehow they made it to La Paz and took some time to modify their cars for the desert crossing. James chose to repair rather than modify and off he went, overtaking both Jeremy and Richard. Once they made it across the border to Chile and began to climb to dizzying heights of about 15,000 feet, progress was slowed. The lack of oxygen meant they couldn't breathe that well for one thing.

Pheww. God Almighty that was close.

Richard took the doors off to save weight, but it got a bit chilly

DAY EIGHT

A shortcut across an active volcano to the Pacific Ocean was chosen and it caused some major problems. The lack of air literally took their breath away and, after much gasping for breath, they decided to descend rapidly just so they wouldn't die. All was well and they gulped in air like fish stranded on a riverbank.

DAY NINE

One last little hurdle though before they could reach the shores. Another small hill in the form of a 2,500 feet sand dune. Richard's Land Cruiser met an untimely death as it rolled and bounced and lost a wheel. Thankfully, Richard wasn't in it. Jeremy and James took off in their 4WDs as Richard galloped after them on foot.

When they got to the ocean an unlikely conclusion was reached. The most **unreliable** car in the world was in fact the most **reliable** car in the world. Jeremy's Range Rover won!

Top Gear Are Here to Help . . . You!

Everyone knows how boring it can be at the airport. Lots of waiting and waiting and more waiting.

Even all the special airport vehicles seem to travel slower than Captain Slow. But what if they were in a race and driven by touring car legends… and Richard Hammond?

And they're off! The catering truck is the surprise lead and quickly takes off down the straight.

Richard's fire truck had eight tonnes of water on board, which slowed him down a bit. The fire truck lagging behind a catering truck? How good would that be in an emergency?

KRAK

The strict no-contact rule Richard had enforced was quickly ignored by the touring car legends. Who can blame them?

46

I can't **see** where I'm going!

Richard had to get back in and restore order. To do this he had a genius idea. He was driving a fire truck!

GA-DANNG

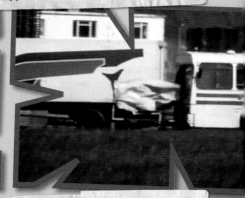

The new track conditions presented a bit of a challenge to the drivers. The bendy bus began to snake all over the track. Where was it going to go next?

Still there was no clear winner so with much regret Richard ordered 'maximum revs' to see what would happen. And everything went crazy.

JANGG

But he forgot about the laws of physics and over he went. Richard was the clear winner!

Now it was a one-on-one race between Richard and the catering truck. And the catering truck driver had a brilliant plan: offload excess weight.

NB: Due to this research you will now only see fire trucks at airports.

RALLY CAR SURPRISE

James flew to the United States so he could jump into a rally car with Ken Block.

He's a man who loves to hone his skills on an airfield and Captain Slow was left speechless aside from 'Oh!' and 'Phwoar!' and the occasional panic.

How to play:

Choose whether to play as Captain Slow or Ken Block. Use coins as counters and place them on the start. The player who can sing the *Top Gear* theme the loudest goes first. Roll a die to make your way through the airfield and see if you find any surprises along the way.

START
Decide to get into a rally car with Ken Block. Roll a 1 to start.

1

2

3

40
See a jump ahead and decide to take it. Fly forwards 5 spaces.

41

42

39

37

38

36
Decide to go back into the airfield to chase Ricky, but take a wrong turn. Roll a 2 or a 4 to move on.

Where the hell are we going *now?!*

FINISH
Congratulations! You've made it. High-five the other player.

35

59

34

VRRRAAAAA

58

33

57

56

55

54

32
See Ricky Carmichael appear and speed up to catch him. Take another turn.

SCREEE!!

27
Next stop is Ken's eyeball spin dryer. You feel dizzy and might be sick. Miss a turn.

26

25

31

30

29

28

48

4

5
Have trouble strapping yourself into the seat and putting on your helmet. Miss a turn.

6

7

8

9
Start the engine and rev until you can't hear yourself screaming with excitement. Only move if you roll a 1, 2 or 3.

10

11

43

44

45

46
Get too overexcited doing 360-degree turns in the dust. Lose visibility. Miss a turn.

47

48

49

12

13
Accidentally nudge an aeroplane as you start off through the airfield. Miss a turn.

14

15

16

That was incredible!

51
Feel overjoyed with happiness that you survived the obstacle course. Take an extra turn and shout 'I'm alive!'

50

53

52

17

Mind the aeroplanes!

18
Screech through the aircraft hangar and pick up speed. Take another turn.

24
Take a shortcut through a fire station but go the wrong way. Miss a turn.

23

22

21

20

19

49

Ode to Top Gear

Using Jeremy, James, Richard and The Stig as inspiration, write your own picture rhyme below.

_____ likes to shout and be the boss

And _____ likes to drive and get . . . .

_____ is short and loves Porsches the most by far

The only thing _____ knows is how to drive a . . . .

What we all know is that _Top Gear_ is . . . .

Especially when  ,  and

are put to . . . .

which is which?

Top Gear asked you to vote for your favourite car company of all time and when it was announced... of course they didn't agree with you.

They voted Lancia. You voted Ford. Just how well do you know your Lancias and Fords though? Match the model names with the pictures below.

The car company that has made the largest number of great cars ever in the history of the world chart

1. Ford
2. VW
3. BMW
4. Jaguar
5. Alfa Romeo
6. Mercedes
7. Audi
8. Land Rover
9. Lamborghini
10. Ferrari

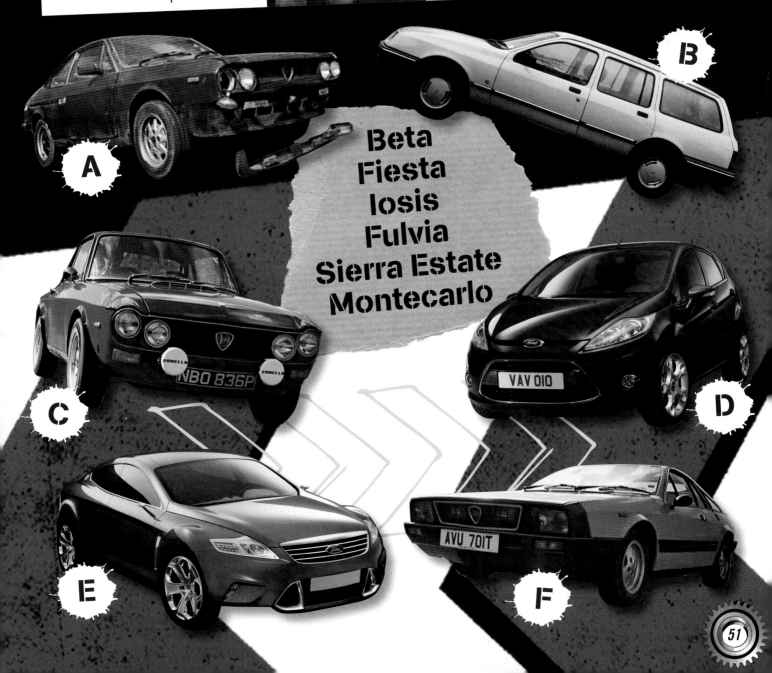

Beta
Fiesta
Iosis
Fulvia
Sierra Estate
Montecarlo

A

B

C

D

E

F

The STIG

True... or False?

The Stig: We know that if you knew what The Stig knew you'd wake up screaming... Every. Single. Day. Luckily, you don't, so all is well. But how well do you know The Stig? Answer the questions below to find out.

		TRUE	FALSE
1	Every time someone uses the word 'mincemeat', the Stig gets 25p.	☐	☐
2	The Stig is convinced that clouds follow him.	☐	☐
3	The Stig is very, very afraid of pigeons.	☐	☐
4	Some say that he once wrestled an elephant to the ground just using the power of his mind.	☐	☐
5	Some say he doesn't understand the concept of queuing.	☐	☐
6	From May 1989 until January 1990, the Stig only ate cheese. As a result, he went slightly yellow for a bit.	☐	☐
7	The Stig thinks that *Star Wars* is a documentary.	☐	☐
8	Some say that if you nibble at his hair it tastes like lettuce.	☐	☐
9	The Stig is one of the world's leading authorities on microwaves.	☐	☐
10	Some say that if he caught fire, he would burn for 1,000 days.	☐	☐

Lancia LOVE

Top Gear votes the Lancia as the best car company in the world. And they're all very special (because that's what their mothers told them). So why exactly did they have so many things go wrong with them? See if you can find these words in the grid below.

> I wanted one more than I wanted my next *breath.*

Rally Championship
Locked brakes
Beta Spyder
Impractical
Scandal
Corrosion
Unreliable
Gamma
Delta
Fulvia
Aprilia
Monte Carlo
Stratos
HPE
Thema
Rust

```
R O M C K F U C O A W V L K X G S L
U E E O X O R U M W R Q F Y A C
S J A R H N S M N Q N Y F D P R G U O
T Z X R F X A E V C T H A X E J O M
H A G O D G N O I E K O Q H S Y L A T R
P I H S N O T U H S T R P D E L C A
G V V I L T O M A P N Y F S B S R P
C L D O M A E D P R A U M D W L
K U H N D E I N T E R L N R A B
R F X W Y Z N Y F A R L N R A K L
D R X M A Z I E A R T E M U E B L
M L S Q I L B L P C X I L L A C T
W B L H Y Z L F G K T Z K S S Z A P Z M O N
Y M O N T E C A R L O I H B C A R L
S O T A R T S P L C L J U E B E X B
L U T O Z N U E O I U E Q I M G T F
T P G H F P F T A B L W J O H A Q P
```

53

Gee-whiz!

Top Gear's Electric Car Masterpiece!

It's all very simple, really. The *Top Gear* team were going to make their very own electric car. James was in charge of the power, Jeremy was in charge of the bodywork and interior, and Richard was in charge of the chassis and the brakes. What could possibly go wrong?

Quite a few things, actually. So they retired Geoff the electric car and went back to the drawing board. Their revised model Hammerhead-i Eagle Thrust was new and improved and it was ready for some tests to see if they could sell it to the general public.

TEST 1

Crash Test

Jeremy was so confident that the Eagle Thrust would pass with flying colours that he decided to use a different sort of crash-test dummy. The *Top Gear* team. But Jeremy had a cunning plan: if they drove at a safe pace towards the brick wall when they crashed, they would all move in slow motion. When they watched it at normal speed it would look like they were actually crashing! Of course, Richard would not sound like a chipmunk and Jeremy would not look he was having some sort of fit. It worked.

GADONK

PASSED

TEST 2

Pendulum Test

This is a test to see how a car would hold up if it were to be side-swiped by a bus or a truck. Not a problem for Eagle Thrust! James suggested they film it backwards. All they had to do would be start at the 'side-swiped' car, run backwards away from the car and then Richard shout, 'Look out!' backwards. (It sounds like **'twah-cool'** if you want to try.) Did it work? Yes!

Drag Race

The team were feeling so confident they decided to have a drag race against a Prius, a G-Whiz, a cyclist and a runner. Even after Richard jumped the starting flag, the Prius managed to pass him. Easily. But that doesn't matter because the main rival was the G-Whiz and guess what? Eagle Thrust beat it! By miles!

PASSED

TEST 4

Comfort and Build Quality Test

Considering it was so roomy, comfortable and had a body built by Jeremy, this wasn't going to be a problem at all. Just a short little drive across some uneven cobblestones. But the weight of James' generator was too much for the chassis and as they bounced along the cobblestones the chimney detached, filling the car with smoke. But the doors didn't fall off. So did they pass? Yes!

PASSED

RRMMMBLL

PASSED

PASSED

Steep Hill Test

A quick run-up and the Hammerhead-i Eagle Thrust shot up the hill… to the starting line. Did it cross over it? Doesn't matter! To keep things fair, they decided to use an **independent driver** to see if the G-Whiz could make it up the hill. This driver – who had no vested interest in the Eagle Thrust – gave the G-Whiz the beans up the hill. And it didn't make it even close. Did the Eagle Thrust pass? Yes, it did!

LK06 JXF

TEST 6

Wind Tunnel Test

Given Jeremy's streamlined design, this test assessing the aerodynamics of the car wouldn't be a problem at all. Of course, the car wasn't the problem. It might've been the operator of the wind tunnel machine: Jeremy. As the winds reached 80 mph the little Eagle Thrust drifted backwards into the fans. **Crunch!** Did it pass? Well, it was hardly the car's fault, was it?

L960 RWY

PASSED

CLANGG

Measuring Range Test

There was only one person who would be suited to testing this eco-car. The Stig's **vegetarian cousin!** Fitted with a green suit, solar panels and Birkenstocks, he looked like he was made for the Eagle Thrust. Sadly, their relationship was fairly short-lived due to a generator exhaust problem. The Stig's vegetarian cousin didn't quite make it out alive. But as this was a minor detail and didn't really impact on the performance of the *car*, the *Top Gear* team gave it a pass.

PASSED

TEST 8

Autocar Magazine Road Test

To keep the identity of the designers of this magnificent vehicle a secret, the iHamm was dropped off to Autocar's headquarters by an anonymous driver: The Stig. When copies of the magazine were delivered to the team, they couldn't wait to hear the shining reviews. But they were terribly disappointed. They wrote that if you bought one of the Hammerhead-i Eagle Thrusts, you could **crash** and there were still a *few* issues meeting general safety rules. What would they know?! **They're only car reviewers!**

FAILED

Just How Clever Are You?

The *Top Gear* team drove an Aston Martin, Lamborghini and a Ferrari to Romania to drive on the world's greatest road built by a dictator (not called Jeremy).

On their journey, they all tried to prove whose car was best with their knowledge and navigational skills. Can you prove your extraordinary grasp of the English language by seeing how many words you can make out of Transfăgărăşan?

I'm *winning* by 1.5 metres. I found it first!

Transfăgărăşan

....

....

....

.... *Nice hat, Jeremy!*

....

....

The Mighty Explorers

Jeremy, Richard and James were possibly the worst intrepid explorers ever to be launched into the Amazon.

The evidence is in the pictures below. Take a long, hard look at the scene, then turn the page and answer the questions.

ARRRGGH!

1. Who is standing on the barge?

....

2. Name the two cars visible on the barge.

....

3. What is attached to the top of the pole on the barge?

....

4. What are the colours of the pole on the barge?

....

5. What colours are the cars on the barge?

....

6. Who has fallen over?

....

A CAR VS. A POSTMAN

A Porsche versus the Royal Mail service should be a shoo-in, right? Perhaps not.

Richard and James travelled for hours and hours and *hours* in an effort to beat a letter that had helicopters, planes, trains and lorries to help it along the way.

> What have they got working on the road? *Tiny mice* that I can't see?

Across

2 What country are Porsches made in?
4 What do they use to keep track of the letter?
6 What country is the letter being delivered to?
7 What kind of stabbed animal did James liken the Porsche to?
8 What form of transport did the car go on?

Down

1 What device was fitted to the letter?
3 What did James entertain Richard with?
5 What kind of office did the letter go to?
8 What does Richard do after he eats his dinner?

But is it Art?

The *Top Gear* team like to present themselves with **challenging** challenges – the more out of their realm of experience, the better. So, taking on the task of producing an art show that would attract 10,000 visitors in a week was a **brilliant** idea!

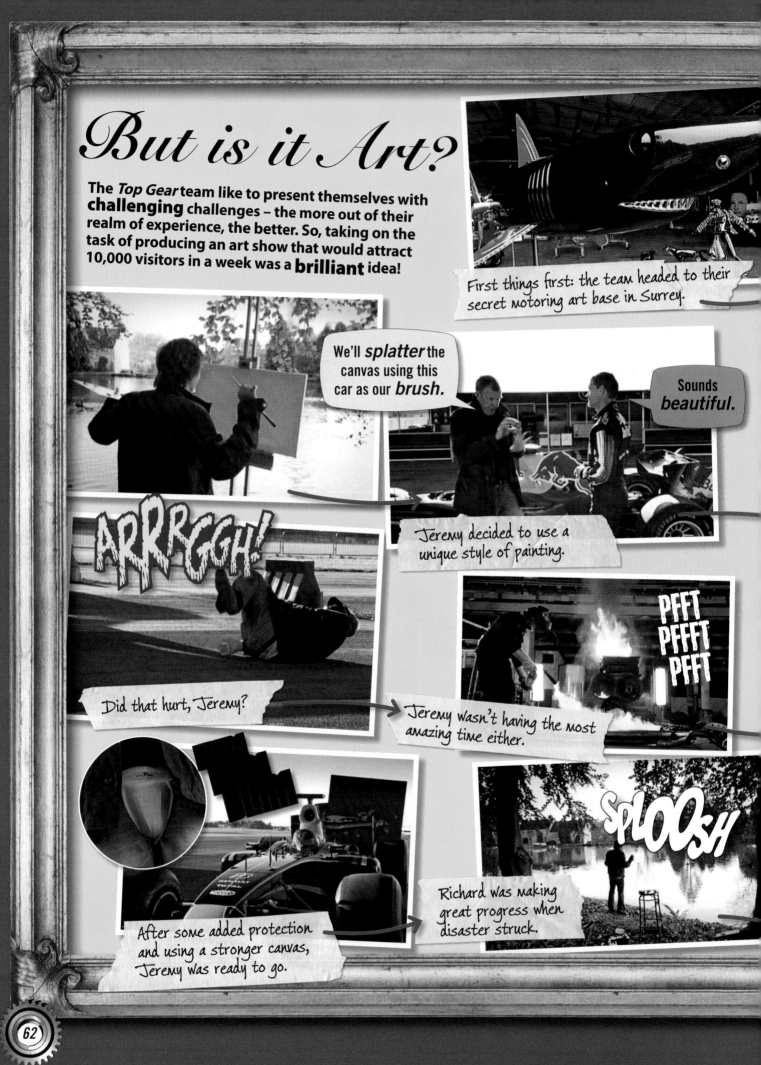

First things first: the team headed to their secret motoring art base in Surrey.

We'll *splatter* the canvas using this car as our *brush.*

Sounds *beautiful.*

Jeremy decided to use a unique style of painting.

ARRRGGH!

Did that hurt, Jeremy?

Jeremy wasn't having the most amazing time either.

PFFT PFFFT PFFT

After some added protection and using a stronger canvas, Jeremy was ready to go.

Richard was making great progress when disaster struck.

SPLOOSH

Make it Happen!

You must be feeling pretty inspired and ready to be creative. Use this space below to create the *Top Gear* car of your dreams.

Try using collage, drawing or stickers to express your deepest, innermost feelings about *Top Gear*. There's some bits and pieces for you to cut out on page 88 to help you.

THE STIG

TOP
GEAR
TECHNOLOGIES

Pondering Power Laps

The Power Lap is one of the highlights of every *Top Gear* show. How fast can The Stig actually make these machines go? And will this be the car that knocks the number one from its spot?

Answer the questions below and the highlighted squares will spell out the maker of a VERY fast car…

1 What make of car had to be fitted with a *Top Gear* spoiler?

2 What model Lamborghini is the fastest around the track?

3 What make of car is one of the slowest on the power lap board? (You'd be surprised.)

4 What's the name of the company that makes one of Richard's favourite cars?

5 Who makes the Scuderia?

6 What make of car was the second fastest around the track at the end of Series 14?

7 What is the name of the kit car that has been around the track?

True or False?

		TRUE	FALSE
1	Because he is so tall, Jeremy is permanently scared of heights.	☐	☐
2	James once had his helmet decorated by a glamour model.	☐	☐
3	Richard once completed a race with a height-challenged man as his partner.	☐	☐
4	James once head-butted a *Top Gear* camera.	☐	☐
5	Jeremy was once hypnotised on television.	☐	☐
6	The Stig was revealed to be Michael Schumacher.	☐	☐
7	James' belt of many things included a shoeshine kit.	☐	☐
8	Richard is terrified of any kind of insect.	☐	☐
9	Every *Top Gear* member has driven the Bugatti Veyron.	☐	☐
10	Pictures of James have been stuck in the 'seriously uncool' section of the Cool Wall.	☐	☐

69

What Will They Think of Next?

It works!

More to the point, what will James May think of next? In an attempt to move unsightly caravans off the road, James invented a caravan airship.

It might not rid the whole of Britain of the caravan but at least they won't be at eye level anymore. Just don't look up.

James did run into a few teething problems with his airship. Find all these words, in order, by tracing a line from one square to the next (no diagonal moves). We've started for you!

Airship	Burnt	Helicopter
Airfield	Headwind	Drift
Caravan	Mayday	Trees
Crash	Airspace	Sideways
Flying	Traffic	Capsize
Sausage	Police	

I believe this is the solution to all our problems!

A	I	R	U	R	N	T	H	E	Y	D
R	I	S	B	U	A	W	D	A	A	A
F	A	H	E	S	S	I	N	D	M	Y
I	P	I	G	A	G	N	R	T	I	A
E	S	H	F	L	Y	I	A	E	R	S
L	A	R	L	O	P	F	F	C	A	P
D	C	C	I	C	C	I	E	E	I	D
R	A	N	H	E	T	T	R	S	S	E
A	V	A	E	I	F	C	S	Y	A	W
O	C	I	L	R	P	A	E			
P	T	E	R	D	S	I	Z			

Seriously Un cool

UN COOL

COOL

SUB ZERO

Lamborghini Murcielago SV

BMW Z4

Pagani Zonda

Nissan 370Z

Ford Focus RS

The COOL WALL RETURNS (again!)

The return of the Cool Wall sparked some disagreements, as per usual, between Jeremy and Richard.

Of course they both acted maturely and didn't go to extreme measures to make sure they got their own way. Draw a line to where you think the cars above are on the Cool Wall... according to Jeremy.

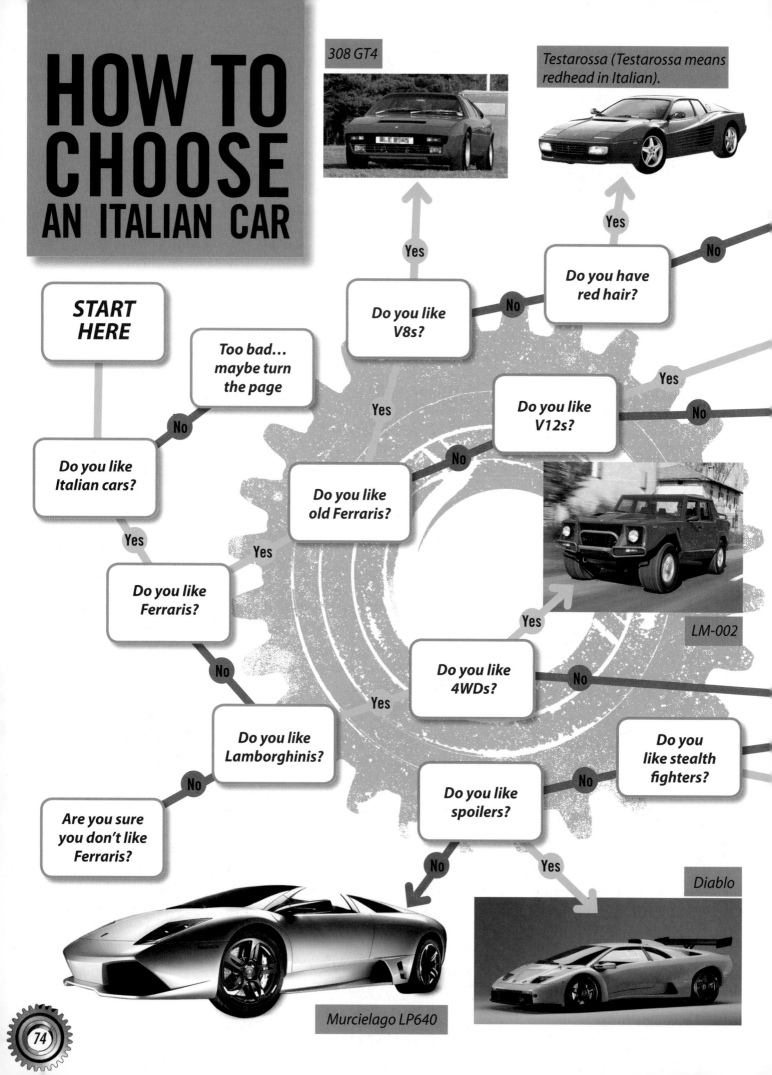

HOW TO CHOOSE AN ITALIAN CAR

START HERE

Do you like Italian cars?

No → Too bad... maybe turn the page

Yes → Do you like Ferraris?

Yes → Do you like old Ferraris?

No → Do you like Lamborghinis?

No → Are you sure you don't like Ferraris?

Do you like old Ferraris?

Yes → Do you like V8s?

Yes → 308 GT4

No → Do you have red hair?

Yes → Testarossa (Testarossa means redhead in Italian).

308 GT4

Testarossa (Testarossa means redhead in Italian).

No → Do you like V12s?

Yes → (LM-002 / 4WDs path)

No →

Do you like 4WDs?

Yes → LM-002

No → Do you like stealth fighters?

Do you like spoilers?

No → Murcielago LP640

Yes → Diablo

LM-002

Do you like stealth fighters?

Murcielago LP640

Diablo

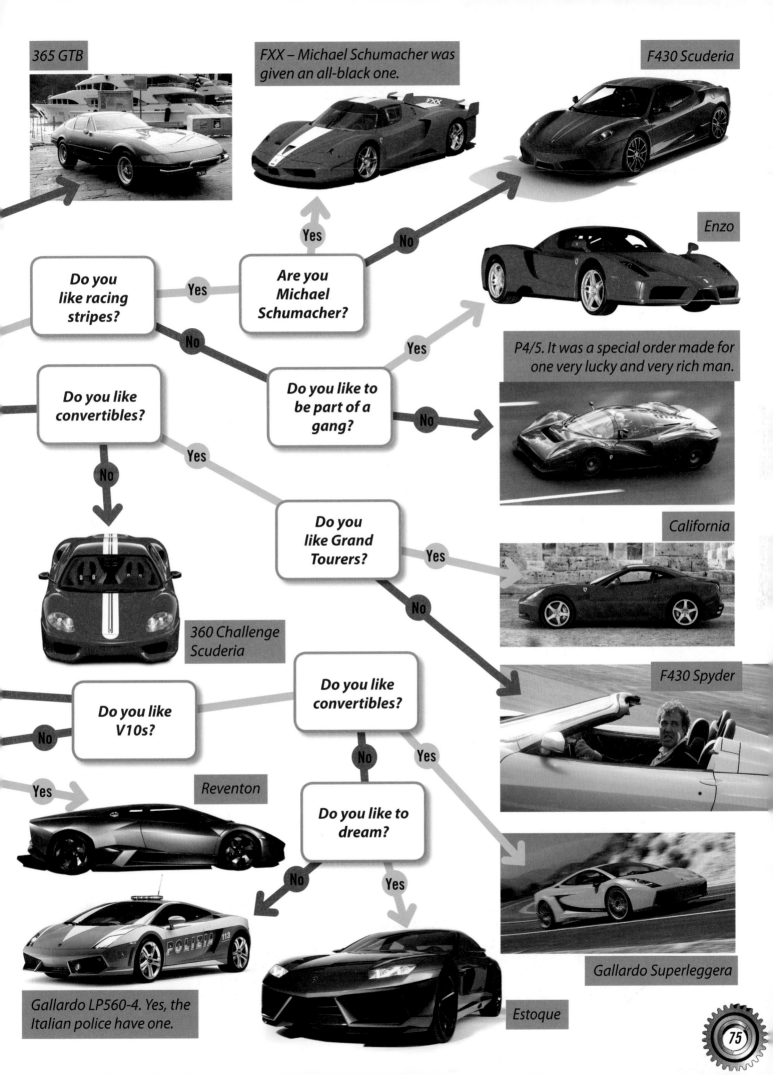

365 GTB

FXX – Michael Schumacher was given an all-black one.

F430 Scuderia

Enzo

Do you like racing stripes? — **Yes** → Are you Michael Schumacher?

Are you Michael Schumacher? — **Yes** → FXX

Are you Michael Schumacher? — **No** → F430 Scuderia

Do you like racing stripes? — **No** → Do you like to be part of a gang?

Do you like to be part of a gang? — **Yes** → Enzo

P4/5. It was a special order made for one very lucky and very rich man.

Do you like to be part of a gang? — **No** → P4/5

Do you like convertibles? — **Yes** → Do you like Grand Tourers?

Do you like convertibles? — **No** → 360 Challenge Scuderia

360 Challenge Scuderia

California

Do you like Grand Tourers? — **Yes** → California

Do you like Grand Tourers? — **No** → F430 Spyder

F430 Spyder

Do you like V10s? — **No**

Do you like V10s? — **Yes** → Reventon

Reventon

Do you like convertibles? — **Yes** → F430 Spyder

Do you like convertibles? — **No** → Do you like to dream?

Do you like to dream? — **No** → Gallardo LP560-4

Do you like to dream? — **Yes** → Estoque

Gallardo Superleggera

Gallardo LP560-4. Yes, the Italian police have one.

Estoque

Supercar

Another world-first for *Top Gear*! Richard took off to Abu Dhabi to race the two fastest production cars of all time. The Bugatti Veyron vs. the McLaren F1.

Not only are they the fastest, they are also two of the most expensive cars in the world. So Richard had to be very careful when testing them and did it on closed roads.

What's so special about these super-luxurious cars, anyway? Let's take a closer look.

Bugatti Veyron

Engine: W16 quad turbocharged
Top speed: 253 mph
Power: 1001 bhp
0-60 mph: 2.5 secs

Richard calls it the 'Concorde of the road' and he'd be right. It broke so much new ground when it was made and still stays on the top of the pile of the super supercars.

The W16 engine is essentially two V8 engines laced together.

To access the top speed, the driver needs to hit the 'Top Speed Key' and go through a series of checks (like whether fresh underwear is available).

There are a total of ten radiators keeping the Veyron from overheating its oil, engine and even its air con systems.

When the car reaches 140 mph, hydraulics lower the car and the spoilers activate.

Michelin had to design special tyres that would cope with such a high top speed.

There is ABS installed on the handbrake, just in case. Phew.

The brakes are made from carbon fibre reinforced silicon carbide, or C/SiC for short.

It's been said that the Veyron will go from travelling at 250 mph to a standstill in less than 10 seconds. Want to try?

Showdown!

McLaren F1

Engine: *V12*
Top speed: *240 mph*
Power: *627 bhp*
0-60mph: *3.2 secs*

In the 1990s, the McLaren F1 was born and was the ultimate road car, even though it is pretty light on gizmos. There is no traction control and no ABS, but that doesn't matter, because it was invented to be the purest driving machine ever made.

Engine bay is lined with gold.

Driving seat is in the middle so you can feel like a F1 racing car driver.

The V12 engine is built by BMW.

The first car to have a body made out of carbon fibre.

A whole new gearbox was invented to survive the torque.

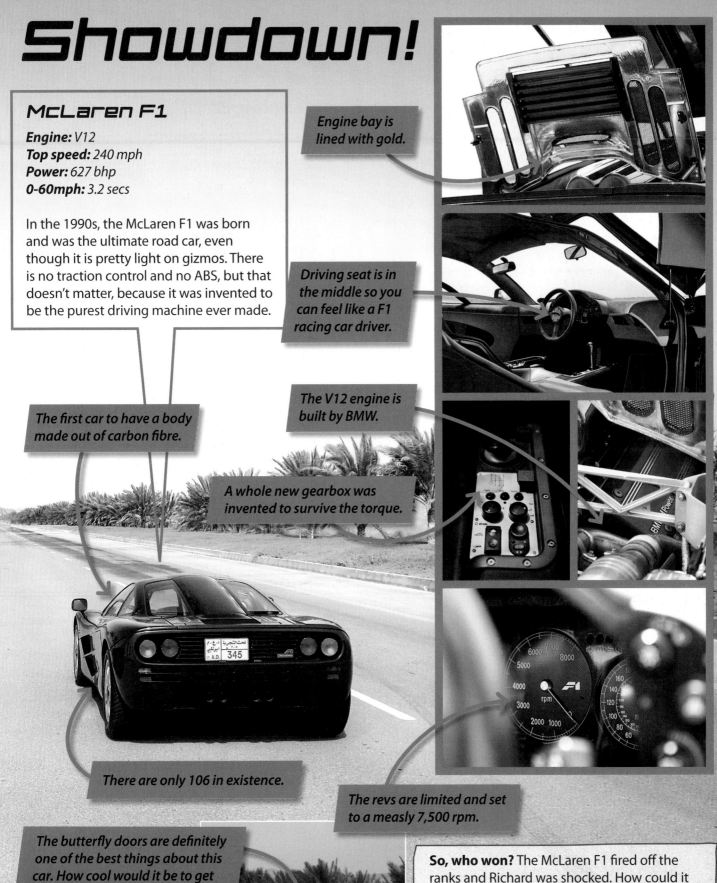

There are only 106 in existence.

The revs are limited and set to a measly 7,500 rpm.

The butterfly doors are definitely one of the best things about this car. How cool would it be to get into one of these at the shops?

So, who won? The McLaren F1 fired off the ranks and Richard was shocked. How could it possibly be streaking ahead? It was time to put the Bugatti through its paces – the foot was planted and the RPMs were high. This is all the encouragement the Bugatti needed to fire past the McLaren F1 and be victorious!

Spot the Difference

Keen eyes at the ready? This game involves spotting... get ready for it...the difference between each set of pictures. Make sure you don't look at the Answers page for hints!

A

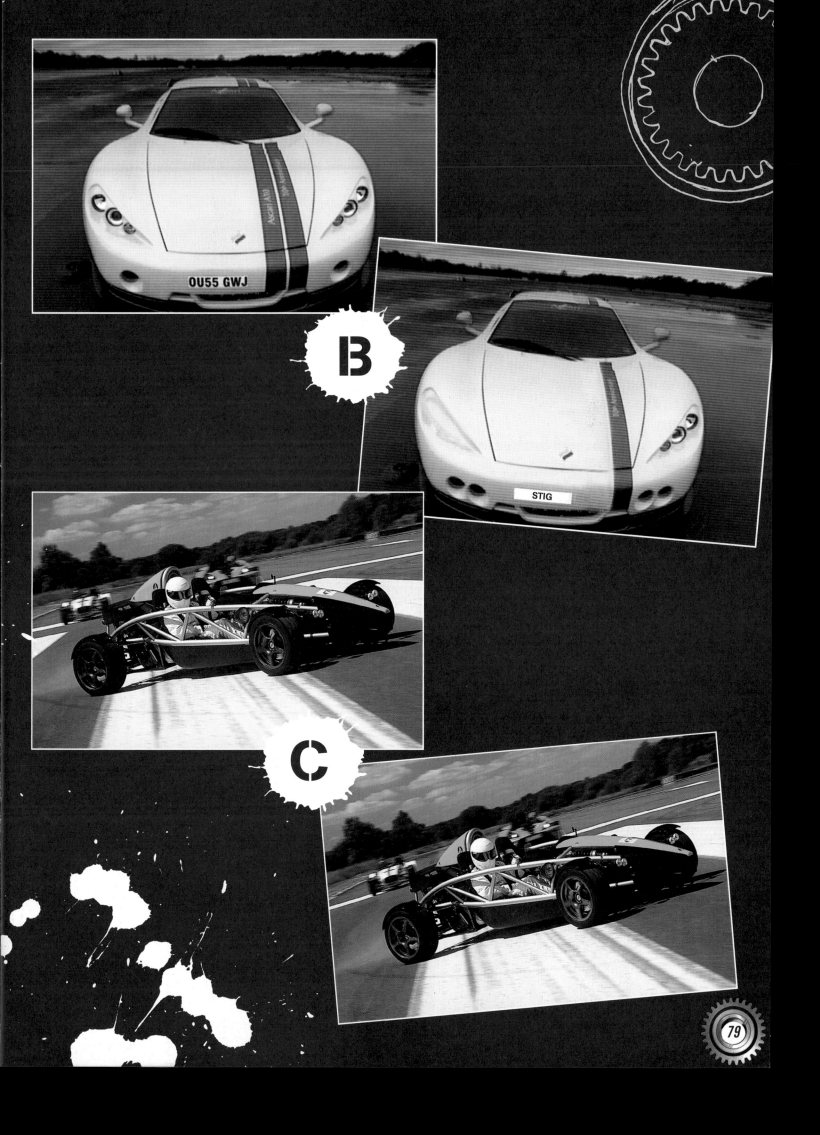

OU55 GWJ

B

STIG

C

79

The Top Gear Awards

These highly anticipated awards are without a doubt delivered with the most glamour and glitz there is – James May wearing a gold lamé jacket.

Injury of the Year

Nominees:

Richard in the Hammerhead-i Eagle Thrust

Jeremy making paintball art

James on a gangplank in Bolivia

Winner:

James and Richard for head-butting a light. Repeatedly

Fastest Star Around the Top Gear Test Track

AC/DC frontman Brian **Johnston** (though the trophy says Brain Johnston – well, it was cheap)

Car of the Year

Volkswagen Polo
Kia Cee'd
Suzuki Alto
Lamborghini Gallardo Balboni

Turn over For the winner…

Idiot of the Year

For delivering the vintage Jaguar to Kings Cross Station four minutes before the Race to the North began, with the keys in the ignition, the engine running – and the door locked…

The Stig!
The Stig was so pleased to receive his prize that he wouldn't give it back.

And so, ladies and gentlemen, the *Top Gear* Car of the Decade *is…*

A car that… just rewrote the rulebook, really. An *amazing* piece of engineering, a genuine Concorde moment.

The Bugatti Veyron

SUPER QUIZ

There's no more mucking around now. Just how much do you know about *Top Gear* really? It's time to find out. Focus your mind – maybe even try channelling The Stig – and give these questions a shot.

1 What car was Jeremy referring to when he said it had 'enough torque to tenderise an elephant'?
a) BMW X5 M
b) Audi R8
c) Noble M600

2 James had some terrifying news. Despite *Top Gear*'s efforts at eradicating caravans, they keep on breeding! How many caravans are now in the UK alone?
a) 500,000
b) 100,000
c) 1,000,000

3 Who was the touring car legend that drove the bendy bus in the Various Airport Motorvehicles Race Challenge Race?
a) Ken Block
b) Richard Hammond
c) Gordon Shedden

4 Why did James call Jeremy an 'apocalyptic dingleberry'?
a) Jeremy bumped his car towards a cliff in Bolivia
b) Jeremy took a car to Australia to see if the glovebox worked
c) Jeremy electrocuted James when making the electric car

5 Which Ferrari will replace the F430 Scuderia Spider 16M?
a) F433 Scuderia
b) 458 Italia
c) Affogato 640

6 What kind of Volkswagen did Jeremy and James have to make an advert for?
a) VW Golf GTi
b) VW Polo
c) VW Scirocco TDi

10 In Bolivia, what special kit did James have on his 'special belt of many things'?

a) Shoe-polishing kit
b) An assortment of flares
c) Sewing kit

7 Where did Jeremy drive a Twingo upside down?

a) In the Renault design headquarters
b) In a sewage tunnel in Belfast
c) In the parliamentary tunnels of Romania

8 What happened to James in Romania during the challenge to find the world's best driving road?

a) His satnav didn't have Romania listed as a destination
b) He was sidetracked by street vendors selling delicious treats
c) He was kidnapped by goat herders

9 What did Jeremy do to the Cool Wall after Richard was trapped on the hydraulic lift?

a) Moved all of the cars that Richard thought were cool to the 'uncool' section
b) Took all the Porsche pictures of the wall off and jumped up and down on them
c) Added photos of Richard to the 'seriously uncool' section

11 When Jeremy played British Bulldogs with the army, how much horsepower did one of their machines have?

a) 2,000 bhp
b, 1,500 bhp
c) 1,001 bhp

12 What is the name of the Lamborghini that hasn't been made yet?

a) Estoque
b) P4/5
c) Miura

13
What did Jeremy do when he road tested the Renault Twingo?

a) Locked The Stig in the boot
b) Drove off the end of a pier
c) Spun off the *Top Gear* test track

14
What was the name of the gallery where the *Top Gear* team exhibited?

a) MOMA
b) MIMA
c) MAMA

15
How many countries did Jeremy visit to do the most expensive car review ever?

a) 4
b) 6
c) 5

16
What kind of car was crashed on the team's visit to Romania?

a) Morris Marina
b) Volkswagen Beetle
c) Dacia Sandero

17
Which Australian actor beat Jamie Oliver in the Star in a Reasonably -Priced Car lap?

a) Eric Bana
b) Russell Crowe
c) Mel Gibson

18
What car did Michael Schumacher take around the test track?

a) Ferrari Scuderia
b) Ferrari FXX
c) Ferrari Enzo

19
What car does rally car driver Ken Block drive?

a) Subaru Impreza
b) Hyundai Accent
c) Skoda Octavia

20
What did Jeremy do at the Majorca Classic Car Rally?

a) Lose his temper and sideswipe James' car
b) Go temporarily insane and overtake a Ford Mustang
c) Drive too fast and overheat his car

Art Parts

Cut out these bits to decorate your
art car on pages 66-67.

If you can't find a die to play a game, here's a much more *Top Gear* kind of solution: a Ken Block Spinner.

1) Cut out this whole page and stick it to some thin card.
2) Cut round the car and the base.
3) Carefully poke a pencil or cocktail stick through the red dots. Ask an adult to help you with the sharp bits.
4) Push a drawing pin through the base from underneath, through the red dot. Tape it in place.
5) Drop a button or small bead over the pin, then the car.
6) It's a good idea to push a bit of cork or eraser over the end of the pin to hold it all in place. (And to stop you receiving a terribly painful and dangerous… er… pinprick.)
7) Game on!

TopGear TECHNOLOGY CENTRE

Super Spinner

1

4

2

9

3

5

Look out for these other great Top Gear titles!

ISBN: 9781405907170

ISBN: 9781405906999

ISBN: 9781405907002

Answers

Page 12: Don't Miss!

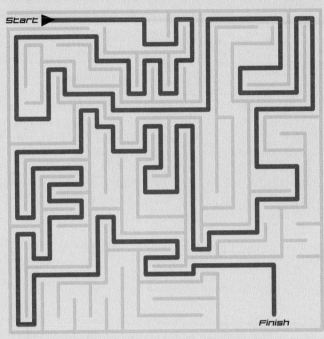

Page 13: Know Your Supercars?

1: a, 2: b, 3: b, 4: a, 5: b, 6: a.

Page 14: Reasonably Fast Stars

1. Boris Johnson, 2. Usain Bolt, 3. Guy Ritchie, 4. Seasick Steve, 5. Tennant, 6. Jimmy Carr. The fastest star is Jay Kay, with a time of 1.45.8

Page 15: Kenny from the Block

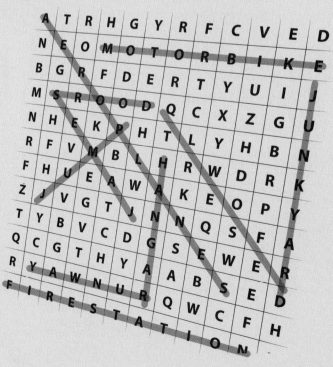

Page 18: The Fast and the Confused

Page 19: Mean Machines

A. Mastiff PPV, B. Jackal, C. Panther, D. Titan AVLB, E. Trojan.

Page 20: Race to the North

Page 21: Power Lap POWER!

Gumpert Apollo: 1.17.1, Ascari A10: 1.17.3, Koenigsegg CCX (with Top Gear spoiler): 1.17.6, Pagani Zonda F Roadster: 1.17.8, Caterham R500: 1.17.9, Bugatti Veyron: 1.18.3.

Page 26: So You Think You Know Your Cars?

1. D, Audi R8, 2. E, BMW X5M, 3. C, Noble M600, 4. A, Corvette ZR1, 5. B, BMW X6, 6. F, Audi Q7.

Page 27: Classic Car Challenge
1. False, 2. False, 3. True, 4. False, 5. False, 6. True, 7. False, 8. True, 9. True, 10. False.

Page 34: How Hard Can it Be?
The route reads 'You lost to a letter.'

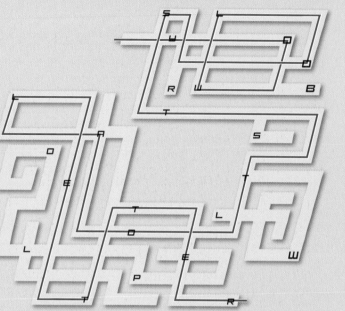

Page 35: Who Said That?
'We then decided to bring a bit of science to the party' – **F, Jeremy**. 'That is the worst-looking car in the whole world' – **C, Richard**. 'I've got my head in a plastic box and everyone can see me!' – **E, Richard**. 'What I'm doing here is helping realise a dream held by many great men' – **D, James**. 'Car makers can learn from this simple system I've adopted' – **A, Jeremy**. 'It's like swimming over a waterfall of double cream' – **B, James**.

Page 36: Where on Earth is Transfăgărăşăn?

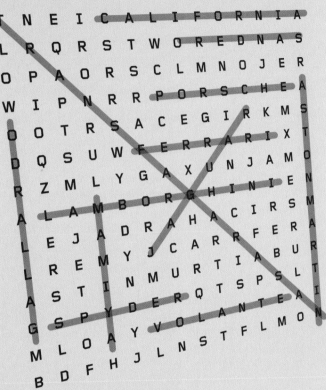

Page 51: Which is Which?
A. Lancia Beta, B. Ford Sierra Estate, C. Lancia Fulvia, D. Ford Fiesta, E. Ford Iosis, F. Lancia Montecarlo.

Page 52: The Stig: True or False?
1. True, 2. True, 3. False, 4. True, 5. True, 6. True, 7. True, 8. False, 9. False, 10. True.

Page 53: Lancia Love

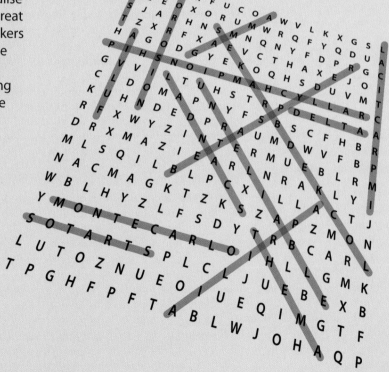

92

Page 58: Just How Clever Are You?

If you manage more than ten words of five letters or more, then you're very clever indeed. Well done. Now go away.

Page 59: The Mighty Explorers

1. Richard, 2. Range Rover and Land Cruiser, 3. A tyre, 4. Red and white, 5. Red and beige, 6. James.

Page 61: A Car vs. A Postman

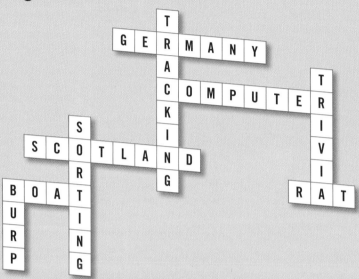

Page 68: Pondering Power Laps

1. Koenigsegg CCX, 2. Murcielago, 3. Aston Martin, 4. Pagani, 5. Ferrari, 6. Ascari, 7. Caterham. The letters spell out 'Gumpert'.

Page 69: True or False?

1. False, 2. True, 3. True, 4. True, 5. False, 6. True, 7. True, 8. True, 9. True, 10. False.

Page 70: What Will They Think Of Next?

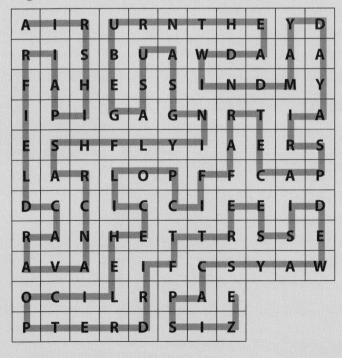

Page 71: The Cool Wall Returns (again!)

BMW Z4: seriously uncool, Nissan 370Z: seriously uncool, Pagani Zonda: seriously uncool, Ford Focus RS: uncool, Lamborghini Murcielago SV: uncool. Remember, this is Jeremy's opinion!

Page 78 - Spot the Difference

Page 80: SUPER QUIZ

1. b, 2. a, 3. c, 4. b, 5. b, 6. c, 7. a, 8. a, 9. c, 10. a, 11. b, 12. a, 13. b, 14. b 15. c, 16. c, 17. b, 18. b, 19. a, 20. b.

93